T·E·M·A·G·A·M·I

T·E·M·A·G·A·M·I

Wilderness and Solitude

PHOTOGRAPHY BY ANDY STEVENS
TEXT BY LYNN BUCKHAM

ACKNOWLEDGMENTS

The real fun for us in preparing this book was in meeting so many interesting people.
We first want to thank all those unsuspecting souls upon whom we descended unannounced,
especially those who graciously showed us their properties and who took the time to chat with us
about their experiences in Temagami. We would also like to extend special thanks to our friends
Heather Parker, Louis Sigouin and Nancy Wood for all of their help in creating this book.
Whether seasonal or permanent, Native or non-Native, new to the area or around for
decades, all share a common bond with this place. It is our hope that together we can maintain its
unique beauty, so that we and those who come after us can continue to have lives enriched by it.

CANADIAN CATALOGUING IN PUBLICATION DATA

Stevens, Andy, 1959–
Temagami: wilderness and solitude

ISBN 1-55046-222-9

1. Temagami, Lake, Region (Ont.) - Pictorial works.
2. Temagami, Lake, Region (Ont.) - Description and travel.
I Buckham, Lynn, 1960–   . II. Title.

FC3095.T39S73 1997   971.3'147   C97-930520-9
F1059.T45S73 1997

Produced by
THE BOSTON MILLS PRESS
132 Main Street
Erin, Ontario, Ontario
N0B 1T0
Tel 519-833-2407
Fax 519-833-2195

An affiliate of
Stoddart Publishing Co. Limited
34 Lesmill Road
North York, Ontario, Canada
M3B 2T6

Editing by James Bosma
Design by Gillian Stead
Printed in Hong Kong by
Book Art Inc., Toronto

Requiem (for the Giants), words and music by Eileen McGann. © Dragonwing Music. All rights reserved. Used by permission.
Available on Eileen McGann's *Turn it Around* CD, distributed by Festival Records 1 800 633-8282.

OVERLEAF: *View from Ferguson Mountain*

TEMAGAMI

Archibald Lampman

Far in the grim Northwest beyond the lines

That turn the rivers eastward to the sea,

Set with a thousand islands, crowned with pines,

Lies the deep water, wild Temagami:

Wild for the hunter's roving, and the use

Of trappers in its dark and trackless vales,

Wild with the tramping of the giant moose,

And the weird magic of old Indian tales.

All day with steady paddles toward the west

Our heavy-laden long canoe we pressed:

All day we saw the thunder-travelled sky

Purpled with storm in many a trailing tress,

And saw at eve the broken sunset die

In crimson on the silent wilderness.

◆ ◆ ◆ ◆

CONTENTS

Old-growth pine (opposite).

◆ ◆ ◆ ◆

TEMAGAMI

◆

A Unique Place

TEMAGAMI means different things to different people. To some it is the best fishing country they have ever found, a much-treasured summer retreat, or one of the last remaining wilderness areas to escape to for a soul-nurturing experience with nature. For yet others it is a home and a highly valued way of life.

What is it that makes this area so attractive to so many? For those who have come to know it well there are many answers. The Temagami landscape is shaped by pervasive rock, majestic forests, clear lakes and streams, unusual islands, and ancient shorelines.

Sunset at O'Connor Island (left). Gulls lifting off (above).

Viewed from the air, chains of sparkling blue lakes ringed with pine stretch in every direction. This network of lakes and rugged hills has been shaped by glacial activity. The larger lakes have been formed by faults or gouged out by glaciers; the smaller lakes and the rivers follow geological fault lines.

Geographically, Temagami is on the top of Ontario and water flows in several directions around it. Lakes north and east of Temagami generally flow east through the Matabitchuan and Montreal Rivers to the Ottawa River. Lake Temagami and lakes southwest flow south via the Sturgeon and Temagami Rivers to Lake Nipissing, and via the French River to Georgian Bay.

The Temagami area also lies on the dividing line between the northern boreal forest and the mixed pine and hardwood forest of Central Ontario. This is especially evident in autumn, when no one colour dominates; the green pine and spruce are speckled with the gold of birch and aspen and the odd red and orange highlights of maple and oak that grow in sunny protected areas.

Temagami is on the fringe of Ontario cottage country that stretches east from Georgian Bay to the Thousand Islands. It is unique as cottage territory because of its particularly unspoiled flavour: much of Temagami looks the same now as it has for hundreds of years. Here there is still wilderness and solitude.

The spirit of Temagami touches all who know the wonder of its shorelines and marshes, the peace of sunsets that envelop the whole sky, the sense of connection at touching trees that have seen centuries pass, even the humbling fury of thunderstorms that rise and transform the lake in minutes into angry heaving darkness.

While there are differing views on how to best manage the vast and beautiful resources this area has to offer, one thing is very clear. Temagami is a unique and special place.

Temagami sunset (left). Sandy inlet (above); Camp Wanapitei is near the top of the photo.

Finlayson Point Provincial Park (above).
The Temagami Boat Livery at Snake Lake (left), is on the edge of the White Bear Forest.

The dog paddle (above).
Silverwater Lodge (opposite).

Temagami harbour (above).
Cottage shoreline (opposite).

Ferns (above).
Caribou Mountain (opposite).

OPENING THE COTTAGE

◆

MAY 2, 1995.

"It's still frozen!" I shout in disbelief over the noise of the outboard motor to my father, who is in the bow of the aluminum boat. He turns and gives me an I-told-you-this-might-happen look borne of sixty-odd years of experience on the lake. I am a little embarrassed, as it had been my idea to make the long drive to Temagami to get to the island this early in the spring, only to find the lake still partially frozen.

As the boat moves toward the edge of the black candle ice, my father catches my impatience and climbs onto the bow to test the resilience of the ice pack. A few moments of bashing the ice with the paddle proves futile. I wonder if he should really be doing this.

Temagami Wilderness Centre at Angus Lake (opposite). Candle ice along the northeast arm (above).

A Narrows Island boathouse (above).
Cathy Dwyer-Smith at the Temagami Garden Centre (opposite).

We try a more practical tactic by exploring leads in the ice. This is a lot easier on both my father and the paddle.

After twenty minutes of zigzagging through channels and crawling through floating slush, we are happy to get onto open water. We chat about how high the water is this year, and pause on the dock to absorb the glorious spring sun, which is as strong as on any day in July. The incredible quiet is broken only by the tinkling of melting ice.

Every year our routine is the same. First we make a cursory check for ice and snow damage, then we take inventory of the trees that have come down over the winter. This year we find only a large cedar against the sleep cabin roof. We quickly move it for later chopping. There never seems to be a lack of firewood around the island. I then jump up to ensure that the roof is undamaged. Finally we open the door to the cottage. Inside, we smell the cold, stale air, and find the familiar evidence that mice have used the place for their winter residence. New traps are set.

Twenty minutes after our arrival, we are amazed to notice that not a trace of ice remains on the lake. A stop in town for a coffee would have made our boat ride a lot easier. But at least we now have a good story to tell when the gang arrives for the Victoria Day weekend.

Next stop is the boathouse. The well-rehearsed process of launching the boat is like a dance, and in fifteen minutes the "big" boat is unstrung from the ceiling and in the water. We double-check that the plug is in, connect the battery, and marvel once again, in a cloud of blue smoke, at how quickly the engine comes to life.

We rest for lunch on the dock, relishing the sun and lack of insects, and talk of projects for the coming summer — replacing dock planks, painting, fixing those leaky taps. We decide not to hook up the water pump, since a few more freezing nights are not out of the question.

Reluctantly, we prepare to leave, but we are satisfied that all is in place for the first long weekend of the summer.

Nesting loon (above).
Wild iris (opposite).

O.N.R. Station (above), originally built in 1906, is the last station of its style still being used by the railway.
Catching the Northlander *(opposite).*

A PORTRAIT IN MOTION

◆

Jim Flosdorf

The land is rock mostly, part of the Canadian Precambrian Shield. The area contains some of the oldest rock on the planet. A thin coating of dirt, sand or clay gives rise to ferns, moss and blueberry bushes, and provides a footing for white birch, red and white pine, and a sprinkling of mountain ash and moose maple. The pines are the most pervasive; the oldest and largest are over two hundred and fifty years old, and over one hundred and twenty feet tall.

In the spring, my island is abloom with white bunchberry, mayflower, clintonia, starflower, and ink moccasin flower. The deep-pink sheep sorrel blooms a little later, as does the wintergreen. In a propitious year, the island is covered with blueberries, and we have to compete with the partridge and her chicks, the gulls, and all the smaller birds in picking the crop.

A boathouse with character (above). Solo cedar-strip canoe (opposite).

Gulls on the shoreline (above).
Witch Bay (opposite).

At the top of a dead standing pine, a young merlin shrills noisily and insistently for one of its parents to bring it yet another small bird. Hummingbirds swoop and dive in aerial combat over rights to the feeders and the bergamot. For a few days of the summer the pileated woodpeckers bring their young around to practice on the trees. When I hear the whisky-jack in the woods, I call him and he comes over to the feeder for meat or beans or fat, whatever I have saved for him (he is actually quite fond of Spam). The last time he visited he brought his whole family with him and showed the little ones how to eat from the feeder. Squirrels, chipmunks, and an occasional mink, porcupine or wood-chuck are my other warm-blooded co-inhabitants.

There is a huge white pine at the end of the walkway up from the boathouse. It bears a lightning scar down its side from a strike about twenty-five years ago. Further up are three giant red pines, and, under these, the main cabin and a sleeping cabin. The cabins are almost fifty years old, and the log siding is weathered and dark.

On a still summer night, the bullfrogs converse at the water's edge, and there is the occasional flash of a firefly. Quick, shadowy movements against the darkening sky indicate that the bats are out collecting mosquitoes. A family of bats lives under the sleeping cabin, and every summer I can hear the brood calling for more milk from its mother.

Right now the sun is descending in the west. It has about an hour left. The wind is low, and there are ripples on the lake. A tame chipmunk has just popped by to eat some after-dinner scraps: a little bread and a plum pit, which he is scraping clean with his teeth. There is a chorus of white-throats and swainson's thrushes.

When the wind is low, the bay forms a natural amphitheatre, amplifying the voices of the birds on the other side. At night, when the loon begins to call, the echo can be heard for miles. It is sometimes eerie, always beautiful.

Muffy enjoys her morning coffee at the Busy Bee (above).
Lake Temagami sunrise (opposite).

Lady Evelyn River.

Novelist Bill Plumstead in his Lake Temagami study (above).
Rocky shoreline (opposite).

COTTAGE TRADITIONS

O ur Temagami summer home is a common thread that runs through our family. Irene wanted to explain this to her young granddaughter Sarah as they sat on the dock in the early morning light, watching the loons dip and resurface. There were so many stories that she had heard from her parents. She had already told them to her own children; now she would begin again with her grandchild.

"The cottage was built in 1906 by your great-grandfather," Irene explained to Sarah, "a few years after he first fell in love with the lake as a young camper at Keewaydin. He had spent a couple of summers building the log cabin and all of its furniture. Your great-grandparents were adventurers in those early years, going on two- and three-week camping trips, usually with the help of a local guide."

Lake Temagami boathouse (opposite). The venerable fiesta ware (above).

Classic log cabin interior (above).
Modern log cottage (opposite).

Cottage life in those days had a sense of formality. Irene would show Sarah the pictures she had of her parents dressed for dinner, her father in a suit and mother in a long dress.

Irene told Sarah about the summers she spent here as a child. She and her brothers were always getting into trouble of some kind. For fun, she remembered, they would sneak into the icehouse, where the family's summer supply of meat was stored. Once inside, they would move the signs around on the tops of the various piles so that, in the evening, mother would be surprised with what she pulled out for supper. The icehouse has long since been converted into a tool shed.

They would also hitch rides on the old steamer, the *Belle of Temagami*, as it cruised past their island. When it eventually docked up the lake, they would climb to the top and fling themselves off into the water. The captain did not approve and was forever shouting at them for their recklessness.

When Irene was a young woman, she went to the dances on Tuesday and Saturday nights at Turners' place on Bear Island. There, all the islanders from the lake would meet. She has many happy memories of those nights.

Irene had missed only two summers on the lake in her seventy-eight years, both due to the gas rationing during the Second World War. She thought back over her years of happy memories: family card games in the evenings, exploring the lake by canoe, building tree forts, singing old songs around the campfire, and building lifelong friendships with the neighbours and their children. Year after year, Temagami called them back.

Sarah let out a squeal of excitement as the loons resurfaced a few feet from the dock and gave a soft eerie cry. "Aren't they beautiful!" she exclaimed in wonder. Irene was pleased with Sarah's obvious enjoyment and hoped that she too would want to carry on the family's Temagami tradition.

Waiting for sunbathers near Axe Narrows (above).
The paddle as art (opposite).

ABOUT RAIN
Jim Flosdorf

Up close the trunks of old pines
shine red and lavender with wetness,
further back, the dripping needles of
white pine, the islands behind, are pale green
and blurry. The sharp shoreline of the far-off shore,
and trees lost in a gray-
green blur, the lake, flat, platinum.

The thing about rain is
the way it separates:
the planes
of trees, of islands,
of hills, of mainland,
with its misty white.

On the roof, rain makes a steady sound,
punctuated by eave-drips on the stovepipe,
it holds me in its waterfall. The only
other voice, the nearby chipping of a bird,
its shrill call piercing the
waves of rain.

The thing about rain is
the way it separates:
the sounds
of outer
from inner
stillness.

It's true, I know, that rain
joins too; it's raining all across Ontario —
but today the rain drives me in-
ward, and I rock in the joy
of its isolation.

Chimo Island garden.

Traditional old log cottage (above).
A cottage on Lake Temagami's southwest arm (opposite).

The cottage kitchen, odd sods and keepers (above).
Pinto Island (opposite).

Chimo Island garden detail (above).
Cassels Lake signposts (opposite).

Buchanan

LAFRENIERE'S
CHALET
←

COOLS
CASSELS

TEUFEL
←——→

DRAKE'S
NEST

BARRETT
BUNGALOW

RON'S
PLACE

Temagami wave at the mine landing (above).
Enjoying free time at Camp Wabikon (opposite).

Under the big top at Canadian Adventure Camp (above).
Cabins at Northwaters Camp (opposite).

REQUIEM (FOR THE GIANTS)

Words and music by Eileen McGann

Four hundred years ago a seed, chance-fallen, grew
In virgin forest land that never white man knew
In woodland silence it rose and flourished
By northern wind was shaped
From earth and sky was nourished

    White pine, silver birch, sing their names in requiem
    Giants of our northern land, we'll never see your likes again

Two hundred years ago, the giants ruled the Shield
'Til white man came and saw the profits they could yield
They fell like thunder and left no trace
But giant stumps that stand as headstones in their place

    White pine, silver birch, sing their names in requiem
    Giants of our northern land, we'll never see your likes again

In north Ontario, some giants still remain
Though few in number now the axe-man comes again
What will you tell them when your children ask you why
Our last remaining forest giants had to die?

    White pine, silver birch, sing their names in requiem
    Giants of our northern land, we'll never see your likes again

And what gives them the right, I ask, to take what's not their own?
To kill a living beauty that four hundred years has grown?
To take and sell our heritage to fill pockets for a day?
And when this crop is gone, what will they say?
And when this crop is gone, the trees are gone,
The wild is gone and the beasts are gone
And the tourists gone and the money gone,
What will they say?

    White pine, silver birch, sing their names in requiem
    Giants of our northern land, we'll never see your likes again

Old-growth trail on Temagami Island (above).
Abandoned telephone line through shoreline reserve, Turtle Lake (opposite).

TEMAGAMI BOATS

◆

Powerboats on Lake Temagami date back to the turn of the century, with the establishment of the Temagami Boat Company. The boat line operated such vessels as the graceful *Belle of Temagami*, the *Aubrey Cousins VC*, and the *Naiad* (fashioned after Queen Victoria's day cruiser, which she sailed on the Thames). The *Naiad* sported a small cannon, which was fired to announce the boat's departure down the lake.

Later, powerful tugs, the *Tom Tom* and the *Andy Milne*, were used by the William Milne and Sons Lumber Company to tow great rafts of pine from every arm of the lake to the jackladder on the northeast arm. The navigation season for these tugs was restricted to after Labour Day and before the Canada Day in order to prevent conflict with pleasure craft.

The Chimo visits the Temagami Lakes Association flea market (opposite). A 1950s cadillac-inspired boat in Temagami harbour (above).

The Andy Milne was quite a sight, with its great upswept bow chugging down the lake, a boom in tow, and the supercharged diesel engine at full throttle to attain the stately speed of one mile an hour. Today, the *Andy Milne* enjoys a more relaxed pace as a pleasure boat on Lake Michigan.

The other great work boats on the lake, though somewhat less majestic, were the barges used by the Copperfields Mine to shuttle equipment, men and ore to and from the mine on Temagami Island. Those barges still provide valuable logistical support today, as they are now used to move sand, gravel and assorted building materials to island construction sites around the lake.

In recent years, a nostalgic interest in the classic inboard mahogany launches that were once common on this lake has resurfaced. Today, replicas, rebuilds and even adored originals can be seen slicing gracefully through the waves. Before aluminum and fibreglass became popular, these inboard launches, and the cedar-strip skiff, were the boats of choice. Many people believe boats made of synthetic material can't match wood for quality of ride. It certainly cannot for aesthetics. Wooden boats require a great deal of maintenance to be kept in good condition. But, according to most owners, it is worth the effort.

Modern craft cover a wide spectrum in style and size. They range from convenient and ubiquitous aluminum and fibreglass runabouts to large cabin cruisers and houseboats with every modern convenience. Whimsical electric boats, perfect for sunset cruises, can also be found on the lake. With future development in Temagami restricted to islands, Temagami residents and visitors will always have a special relationship with boats.

Jerry Burrows's Ketch III *(opposite). Bill Crofut's electric boat* Erika *(above).*

Temagami harbour (above).
1920s Greavette *replica near Sand Point (opposite).*

There aren't many towns where you will see pedestrians like these. A Keewaydin section doing the Temagami portage (above).
Looking north from Camp Wabun (opposite).

CATCHING THE BIG ONES

◆

Many cottagers and homeowners in the Temagami area have dusty old photo albums that contain cracked and faded pictures of spectacular strings of fish. Old-timers tell us that thirty-pound lake trout were once common and that supper could be caught during a ten-minute paddle around the island.

Today it requires dedication, knowledge and sophisticated equipment to consistently land the big ones. A good guide helps too. Thirty-pound trout, though not as common, arc still caught on the lake every year, and, when the walleye are biting, it's still a thrill to catch your limit and enjoy the best tasting game fish around.

Casting at Bell Island (opposite). Tackle shed (above).

"Without a personal visit to Temagami, no one has any idea of the amount of pleasure that is expressed in this one word, and versatile language is not subtile enough to impart an adequate description of its natural beauties and the story of its fourteen hundred odd islands in Lake Temagami, the principle lake of the district, and its thousand and one smaller lakes within a comparatively small area, holding forth unlimited attractions to the canoeist and lover of the rod and gun."

From *Souvenir View*, published and distributed
by the Canada Railway News Company in the early 1900s.

Dropping a line near Camp Adanac (above).
Landing a Lake Trout near Chimo (opposite).

Keeping the fish population strong has become a challenge, but the Temagami Fish Improvement Program, thanks to the dedication of government biologists and local volunteers, has helped immeasurably. Each spring, walleye from Net Creek are netted to retrieve the eggs, which are then nurtured in the hatchery until, as young fish, they can be returned to local lakes.

But the nature of fishing has also changed; no longer is the goal simply to fill the boat. Instead, many anglers are happy to match wits with bass and enjoy the competition of the annual bass tournament. Catch-and-release is also a popular way for people to enjoy the challenge of catching a fish, and then return it to the lake.

An important part of fishing is simply being on the water to enjoy the sights and sounds of nature. What a perfect antidote to our hectic modern world, to breathe fresh clean air, watch the sun slowly set, and listen to the loon's haunting cry.

Casting near Ship Island (above).
Boat Line Bay Marina (opposite).

The Temagami Lakes Association flea market.

GHOST CAMP

◆

on Lake Temagami

On Gull Creek, down the southwest arm of Lake Temagami, there stands a testament to Temagami's logging heritage. The ghostly buildings located here are the remnants of an old logging camp built in the early 1950s and used primarily as a drive camp until the late 1960s.

Log drives were used extensively on the rivers of Quebec but were less common in the Temagami area. The Sturgeon, Montreal and Matabitchuan Rivers, however, were all used at one time for driving logs.

Fog enshrouds the old-growth forest (opposite). Wm. Milne and Sons' log-drive camp at Gull Creek (above).

On a small waterway like Gull Creek, a log drive was a labour-intensive endeavour. Each spring, lumberjacks would spend several weeks corralling the logs cut around Gull Lake over the winter and moving them to the east end of the lake. From there, with a series of dams that can still be seen, the water level was manipulated to allow the pine to float down the rocky creek to Lake Temagami.

Once on the big lake, the logs were towed by the *Andy Milne* and the *Tom Tom* across the hub and up the northeast arm to the jackladder. A jackladder was used to lift the logs from Lake Temagami into Turtle Lake. They were then sent to the mill on Link Lake. After this practice was stopped, Turtle Lake was drained in order to allow the open-pit excavation of iron ore at the old Sherman Mine site. The jackladder is now barely standing, and since the mine is now closed, Turtle Lake has slowly refilled to its former level.

Careful exploration of the old Gull Lake camp is an interesting way to spend an afternoon. A scenic trail begins in the shoreline reserve, where huge old-growth pine hint at what the entire trail must have been like before the timber along this route was logged. It is reassuring to see young pines thrive along the trail. About a half a mile farther stand the weathered old bunkhouses. The barn and the blacksmith shop have long since collapsed and grown over.

During the life of the camp, Milne and Sons made the transition from the use of horses to mechanized operations. The truly observant can find clues to both eras of operation. Daisies, clover, and cow vetch are a few subtle remainders of the horse era. These meadow weeds found their way here in bales of straw brought in to feed the horses.

Cynthia Knudsen, Northwaters Camp (opposite). Summer fun (above).

Camp Wabikon C.I.T.s (councillors in training), (above), and cabins (opposite).

Artist Valerie Hostetler paints the Lake Temagami shoreline (above).
Tying up at Loon Lodge (opposite).

THE BEAR ISLAND POWWOW

◆

The formal ceremonial kickoff to the traditional powwow on Bear Island is the Grand Entry. The hot sun beats down on the several hundred cottagers, tourists and townspeople who are gathered around the edges of the circle to witness the event. To the rhythm of slowly beating drums, the First Nations war veterans step into the powwow circle, carrying the flags of Canada, Britain and the United States. They are dressed in their veteran uniforms, and their faces are stern and proud. Following them are other elders and dignitaries, then the costumed dancers in a line. The parade is made up of approximately seventy, including even very small children.

The Bear Island First Nation Powwow

◆ ◆ 83 ◆ ◆

Dancers have come from all over Ontario and beyond to participate in the weekend-long ceremony. All of them wear different costumes related to the dances they will later perform. Over the course of the next several days, each set of dancers will have a turn to dance the circle.

The slow, solemn procession moves in unison into the powwow circle and then clockwise around the sacred fire, which is located in the centre under an arbour of cedar boughs. The sacred fire is considered the symbolic window to the spirit world, the Natives' ancestors and the Great Creator. As such, it is a place to pray and give thanks. The fire is fuelled by tobacco, sweet grass, cedar and sage, and the smoke is viewed as a visual sign of the Creator receiving the prayers. During the powwow, Indian drummers and singers huddle next to the fire to make the traditional music that accompanies the dancers. Tents have been set up around the outer circle, where many of the dancers and visitors stay.

After the first few introductory dances, the group dances begin. Men and women perform traditional dances separately. The costumes include hunting and war regalia. Many individuals dance to express their own animal spirits, and they are dressed accordingly.

The male grass-dress dancers begin. Their dance originated from the Plains Indians but has been widely adopted by other Native traditions. Legend has it that the elders would ask the young men to dance first and thereby pat down the grass in order to make way for the rest of the dancers. Their costumes are very colourful — instead of real grass the fringes are now made of brightly coloured string.

The women jingle-dress dancers are the most dramatic.

Powwow jingle dancer.

Women and girls of all ages dance into the circle, their dresses covered with many small bells. As they dance, the bells jingle to the beat of the drums. Traditionally this dance was used as part of healing ceremonies.

Finally the fancy dancers have their time in the circle. These are the most recent additions to the powwow. Although they dance to traditional music, their costumes are more modern. Small girls swirl their shawls in elaborate dance moves. Many young people participate in this type of dance.

The air is informal and the mood infectious. Many from the crowd join in as the groups dance around the circle, and small children show their pleasure and pride in their costumes. Spectators come and go throughout the weekend, docking their boats at the Island's main docks and walking toward the sound of the beating drums in the centre of the island. Indian and local handicrafts are sold, and refreshments are provided by the Bear Island First Nation.

Originally, powwows were gatherings in which people met to socialize and trade. While this remains true today, these festivals now also celebrate Native heritage. Powwows provide opportunities to promote understanding and pride in First Nations traditions among Natives and non-Natives alike. In 1994, the Bear Island First Nation took this to heart by organizing its first powwow, as a means of pulling the community together in working for a common purpose. The Bear Island First Nation met its goal. On this fine summer day it provided a festive opportunity for people of all backgrounds to gather together to celebrate traditions, to learn and to have some fun.

Artist Hugh Mackenzie (above).
Caribou Mountain Fire Tower, White Bear Forest Trail (opposite).

St. Simon's Anglican Church (above).
Boardwalk in the White Bear Forest (opposite).

CANOEING IN TEMAGAMI

◆

Doreen Dixon

A canoe can be many things. My canoe is a time machine. It removes me from the maelstrom of contemporary urban life and takes me far away to another time, another world, another life. Anyone who has canoed on a perfectly still summer day, suspended between heaven and earth on a mirror-calm lake, will understand why I say this. I enjoy the challenge of a hefty headwind, especially when the sun arcs off the dancing waves and turns the spray to diamonds. I revel in the excitement of chasing down a river that runs and laughs and tugs ever faster. It is as though we are transcending the normal human role of pariah in nature when our craft moves so sweetly and silently that we can drift amongst the loons and mergansers and moose as if we belonged there.

Campsite at Cross Bay (opposite). A peaceful paddle in a cedar and canvas canoe (above).

Once a year, my husband and I take the canoe into the wilderness. With the constraints of a job, two weeks is all we can manage at a stretch, and what a glorious time it is! No alarm clock, no stoplights, no telephones, no appointments, no obligations. Just the simple joys of eating when we are hungry, sleeping when we are tired, and waking every morning refreshed and invigorated. And the quiet .... It is not until I have been in the bush for two days that my ears stop ringing and I begin to hear the silence — the sigh of the wind in the trees, the whisper of the water on the rocks, the gentle conversation of the birds. Out there, I have heard the trees breathe and the aurora borealis crackle.

Our favourite destination is Temagami, with its incredible network of *nastawgan*, ("ancient canoe routes"), and its rock cliffs, pure water, and incredible variety of birds and animals. Our first trip to Temagami was prompted by our son, who, as a fourteen-year-old boy, had been transformed by a ten-day trek with a camp. He returned ten pounds heavier, two inches taller, and speaking in a voice about an octave lower than when he had left. He had become a confident young man.

"There's nobody in Temagami," he said; so that's where we wanted to be! He had been on the Golden Staircase (the north and south forks of the Lady Evelyn River) and told us that it was both rugged and beautiful. We soon found out for ourselves. The golden staircase boasts sixteen portages — with cliffs and mountainsides — in a route that takes about two days. Words can't describe the sense of accomplishment we felt at the completion of each portage.

That first experience in Temagami was more than a physical challenge. It was an awakening. We survived the next fifty weeks by reliving our adventures — talking about the beauty of the place, dreaming of the silence and sweet air and water — and planning our next trip.

We have since had seven seasons in Temagami, each year taking a different route and enjoying a different experience. Some years we have been lazy, travelling shorter distances or taking routes with fewer portages. Other years, we have tackled lengthy routes filled with long and often arduous portages. Admittedly, as we age, there are times when the way seems too long and rugged, the bugs seem unnecessarily aggressive, and the weather leaves much to be desired. But Temagami has never disappointed, from the first long-awaited sniff of fragrant air after hours on the highway to the excitement of piling the gear into the canoe at Mowat Landing, from the first few wobbly dips of the paddles as we head for the dam and the first portage to the quickly regained rhythm as we put miles between us and civilization.

I have favourite places and memories in Temagami — the magical vista of Lady Evelyn Lake, the rocky campsite that looks down on Sucker Gut Lake, the dance of the loons at peaceful Bergeron Lake, the solitude of Skull Lake with its private island camp, days spent lounging in the sun at the quiet end of Anima Nipissing, the secret passages in Sharp Rock Inlet, and the north arm of Lake Temagami. The old-growth forest on Obabika Lake took us three tries to reach, and it was truly worth the effort. It is a cathedral, a place of peace and solitude, of ancient worship.

Temagami is a gift — one of the finest canoeing areas in the world. We hope to be able to enjoy it for many years to come.

Camps from across Ontario canoe in Lake Temagami (opposite).

I Watch the Lake Breathe
Jim Flosdorf

I watch the lake breathe
its long, slow breaths
as the storm roars
and the wind-swept rain makes
a furious dance on wavelets,
shifting, random patterns
splashing and bubbling on the wave-tossed lake

I watch the lake breathe
its long, slow breaths
as the waves splash in
driven by the roaring wind
while a family of ducks
slips and bobs on the surface
seeking a sheltered cove
on the wave-tossed waters

I watch the lake breathe
its long, slow breaths
as the water lifts,
piled by the wind,
then subsides in a lull,
while the long wave
retreats to the lee shore
then builds again to return

I watch the lake breathe
as the wave-tossed waters
lift and fall,
slow, rocking,
from shore to shore
the long wave
driven by the raging wind
in long, slow breaths

Lake Temagami sunrise.

Portaging a vintage Peterboro canoe at Divide Lake, near the Lady Evelyn River (above).
Lake Temagami's northeast arm (opposite).

Temagami Canoe Co.

CANOE MAKERS
Jim Flosdorf

Quickly, deftly out of the steam chest
a rib extracted,
and with a hasty grace
they bend the supple wood
over the mold and tack it down,
over and over, growing skeleton,
nailing it to backbone,
in the old way

Muscle and tissue planks lift off the mold
like a dragonfly slipping from its chrysalis,
a skin grows, breathes again.
As it swims among brother
pike and bass, cedar and ash,
they nod to each other,
exchange greetings.

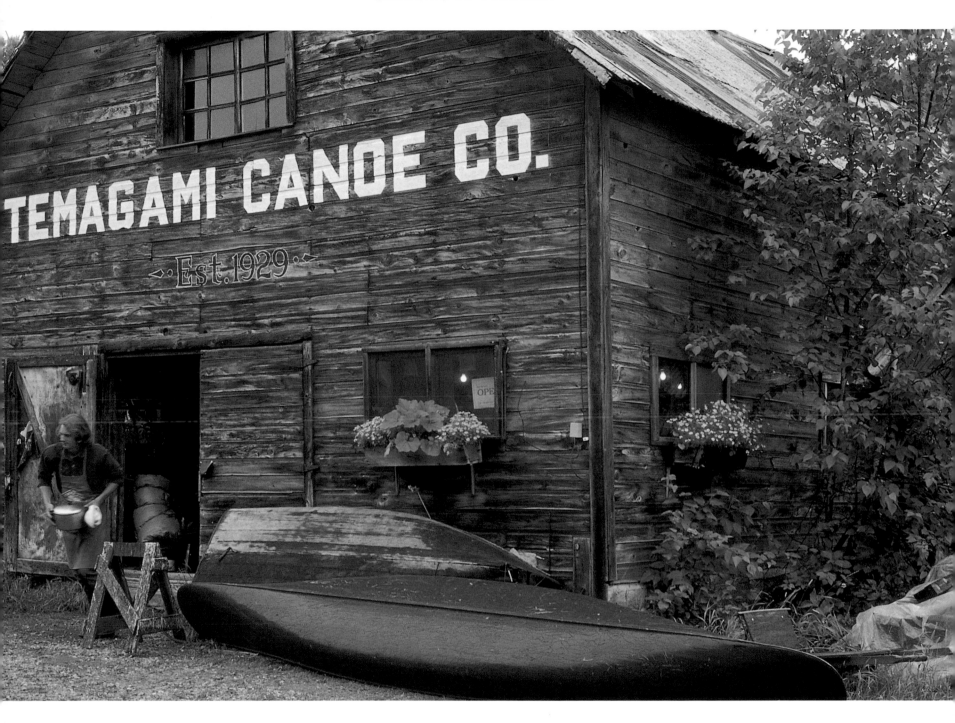

THE CANOE TRIP

◆

Jim Flosdorf

The canoe trip has a special meaning that is deeply ingrained in Canadian culture. It is an annual ritual that is reenacted each summer. For many, it is an event that was first experienced in camp as a teen.

Early Canadian history was shaped by the canoe; it was only by canoe that the land could be explored, mapped and traversed. Until the advent of the bush plane, the canoe was still the only means to enter much of the back country. For the aboriginal traveller, who taught it to the prospector, fur trader and voyageur, it was the preferred means of travel for more than half the year.

Helen Falls on the Golden Staircase, Lady Evelyn River (opposite).
Canoe on shore, Lake Temagami (above).

In an essay entitled "The Soul of a Mountain" (*Copperfield*, volume 5, 1974), Hugh Stewart, under the pen name Grey MacPherson, wrote the following: "In many ways the voyageur is the prototype Canadian folk hero. In no other country will you find voyageurs and in no other country has the canoe and skill in its use been so vital to trade and life."

Today, the canoe trip has become an annual pilgrimage, a reenactment of that early history of the land. Few other countries can boast such a rich and accessible legacy, for the Canadian can take a canoe across the ancient portages, or *nastawgan*, and tread on stones already worn by centuries of travel.

Hugh Stewart further wrote: "I do not feel very close to Canadian history when I visit the National Library and Archives in Ottawa, I do, however, when I paddle through Northern Ontario and realize just what a feat it was to construct a railway through the Canadian Shield." One night on a canoe trip on the Lady Evelyn River, sitting on a rock overlooking Centre Falls, puffing reflectively on our pipes, and speaking in quiet tones just loud enough to be heard over the roar of the falls, Hugh shared this same insight with me.

Eskers campsite, Lady Evelyn Lake (opposite).
Lady Evelyn River (above).

Centre Falls Portage (above).
Dawn, Lake Temagami (opposite).

Centre Falls, Lady Evelyn River.

Lady Evelyn River (above).
O.N.R. tracks just south of Temagami (opposite).

Road to Cassels Lake (above).
Old-growth trail, Temagami Island (opposite).

FACES
Jim Flosdorf

New faces begin to
appear in the forest
as autumn sneaks in:
tints of gold
edge birch, poplar, and cedar
like sunburn, where the sun
strikes most —
highlighting —
funny men or beasts
who talk in a breeze
or fly to pieces in a wind
reappear when all is still —
rain makes them droop
and weep.

The faces, when leaves fall,
will be gone
but back again next year,
slightly changed —
only beaver or man, wind or fire,
make rapid changes in the bush —

and the cedar stays all winter.

WINTER CARNIVAL

◆

After an absence of twenty-three years, the grandfather of all winter carnivals made a triumphant return in 1996. Believed to be the first of its kind in Ontario, Temagami held its first winter carnival in 1958, from which time it ran annually until 1973. It featured such unique events as tea boiling contests, snowshoe baseball and log chopping competitions. There were also the very popular snowmobile and dogsled races. In the early years, the carnival had a distinctly local flavour. It was great to watch friends and neighbours compete in fun, without the benefit of extensive training or sophisticated equipment.

Log sawing (opposite) and the five-legged race (above) at the Temagami Winter Carnival.

Loon Lodge, Lake Temagami (above).
Bear Island tug-of-war team, Temagami Winter Carnival (opposite).

Temagami was a much busier town in those days. The two mines and two sawmills spawned natural rivalries that were heightened during the winter carnival, when community spirit was at its peak. The local curling club, with its frost-covered walls and natural ice, was the social centre of town and always hosted a spirited bonspiel at carnival time.

After a while, the Temagami Winter Carnival began to draw tourists. But, other communities began to hold their own carnivals, and soon nearly every town in the North had one. As a result, small towns like Temagami inevitably found they could not compete with the resources of larger centres, and their carnivals faded from the scene.

But now the Temagami Winter Carnival is back, featuring Temagami classics such as the ice castle, tea boiling and bannock baking competitions, as well as log sawing, tug-of-war and snowshoe baseball. Along with the return of the carnival has been a renewed sense of community spirit.

WINTER WEEKEND

◆

Winter guarantees an abundance of snow in Temagami, which makes it a wonderful time of year to enjoy the area. Popular activities include snowmobiling, cross-country skiing and even dogsledding. My favourite is cross-country skiing. For those of us who do not have the luxury of a plowed ice road or a snowmobile, cross-country skiing is our means of getting to the cottage in the winter. The weekend's provisions are hauled behind us on a toboggan or carried in packsacks. After digging out the front door, starting the fire in the stove, and chopping a hole in the ice for water, we are settled in and the skiing can begin.

Smoothwater Outfitters, James Lake (opposite).
Cross-country skiing at Finlayson Point Provincial Park (above).

Fresh, clean snow can transform even familiar summer trails into magical places. Tree trunks sink into the bed of snow and create patterns of long blue shadows across the trails. Snow-covered pine boughs arch overhead in a canopy, and all around us the place feels new. The pines are more prominent now, frosted with snow against a deep blue sky. Without the foliage of deciduous trees the forest seems more exposed and vulnerable. This greater visibility gives us a more intimate appreciation of its very composition and structure.

Gone are the distractions of summer: no mosquitoes or outboard motors or summer maintenance projects. Instead are cold, crisp, cloudless days of brilliant sunshine on glittering snow. But the biggest change from summer is the overwhelming silence. There is less human activity, and what little noise we do make is absorbed by the snow.

We swiftly skim along the undulating trails through the forest. Sometimes, when we want to leave the trail, we abandon our skis for snowshoes. We finally reach our small secret lake. The frozen bogs and swamps allow us to reach this place, which lies isolated from human contact all summer long. Each year, when we first come upon it, it feels like a new discovery.

Standing still on the tiny lake, we can hear the wind in the trees. This must be why they are called the whispering pine. A gentle wind scatters the snow from the branches in random display. Signs of wildlife are everywhere. The lonely call of the loon has been replaced with the strangely melodic song of the blue jay. Tracks of rabbit and fox are etched on the frozen terrain. We even see a couple of wolves frolicking on the far side of the lake.

After the hard work of the trail, we ski across the lake to an exposed rock, its snow blanket melted by the March sun. We sit in the warmth, refresh ourselves with cold juice, and reflect on the beauty and silence around us.

Dogsledding is enjoying a comeback (above).
St. Ursala's, Bear Island (opposite).

Skyline on Lake Temagami.